PAUL CARDALL

PIANO | VOCAL | GUITAR

THE Broken MIRACLE

T0066211

ISBN 978-1-70513-345-3

Visit Hal Leonard Online at
www.halleonard.com

www.paulcardall.com

Contact us:
Hal Leonard
7777 West Bluemound Road
Milwaukee, WI 53213
Email: info@halleonard.com

In Europe, contact:
Hal Leonard Europe Limited
42 Wigmore Street
Marylebone, London, W1U 2RN
Email: info@halleonardeurope.com

In Australia, contact:
Hal Leonard Australia Pty. Ltd.
4 Lentara Court
Cheltenham, Victoria, 3192 Australia
Email: info@halleonard.com.au

A BLUE BABY

By PAUL CARDALL

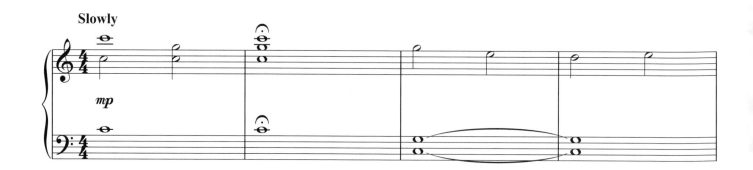

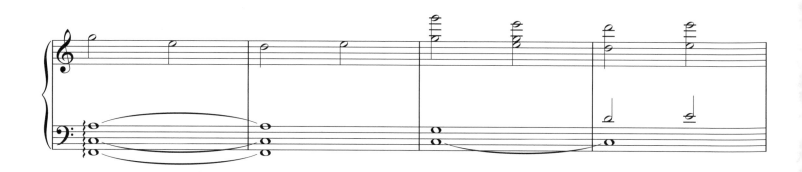

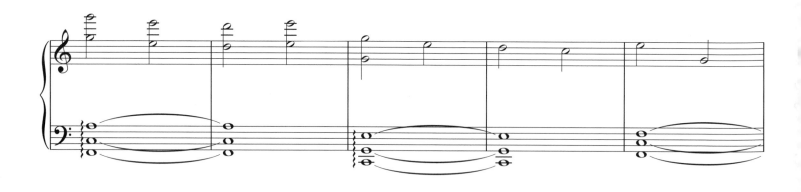

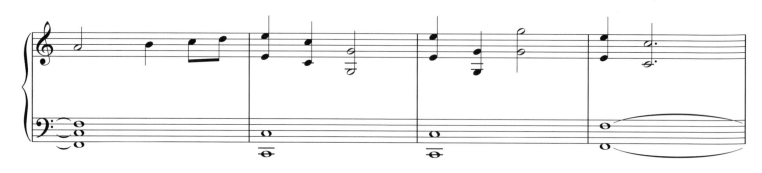

MOTHS & BUTTERFLIES

By PAUL CARDALL

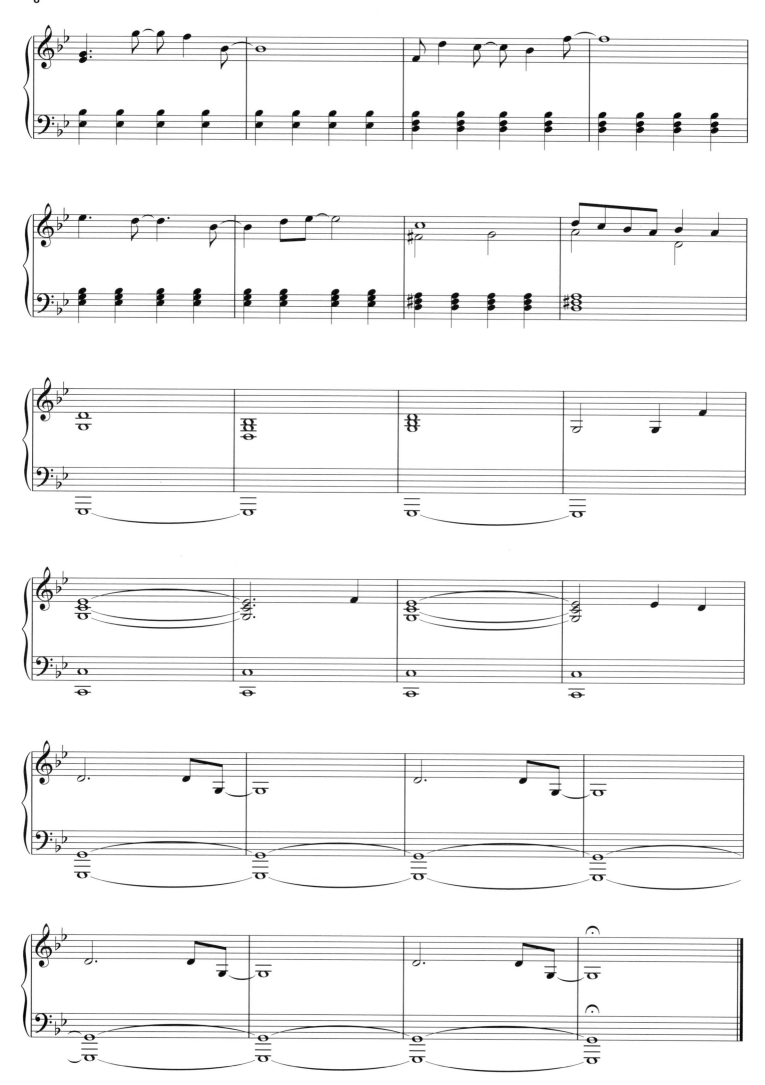

I KNOW IT HURTS

Words and Music by PAUL CARDALL
and TYLER GLENN

THE MAN WITH HALF A HEART

Words and Music by PAUL CARDALL
and KEIFER THOMPSON

Moderately slow, in 2

My life has been one strug - gle and an - oth - er.

Roads with more dead ends than I can count.

I have doubt - ed ev - 'ry - thing, who I was, what I

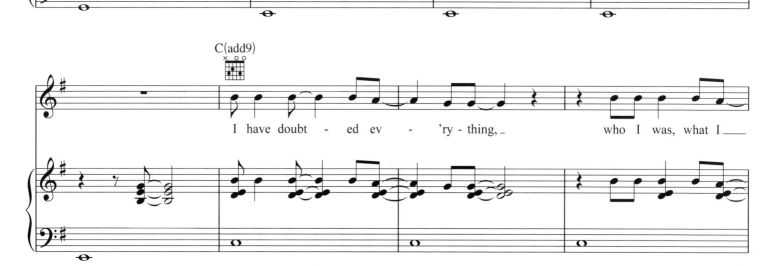

FAMILY

By PAUL CARDALL

Slowly, expressively

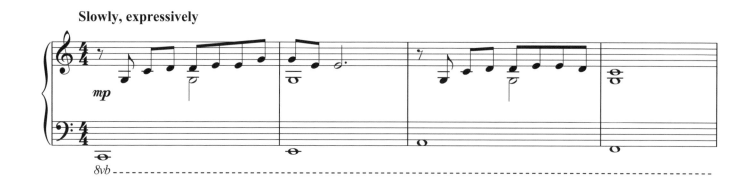

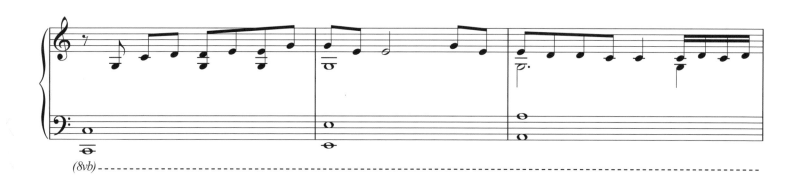

Moderately, more steadily

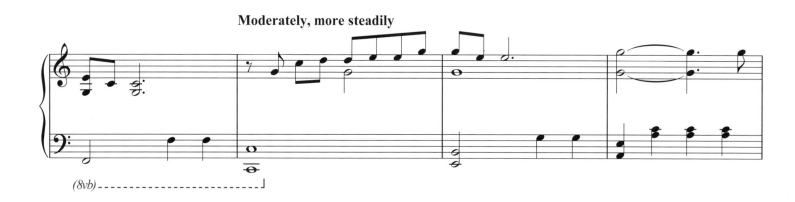

GOD & RELIGION

By PAUL CARDALL

A BEAUTIFUL MIND

By PAUL CARDALL

OUR CHILDREN

By PAUL CARDALL

Moderately, expressively

ALL I SEE IS SNOW

Words and Music by PAUL CARDALL
and KEIFER THOMPSON

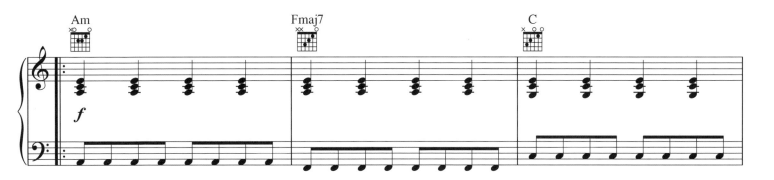

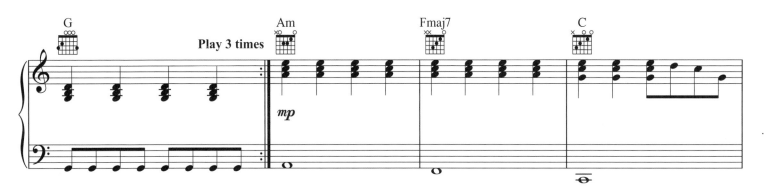

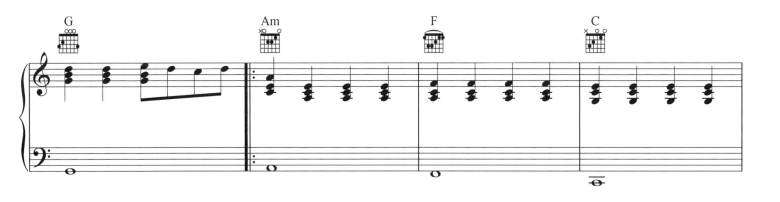

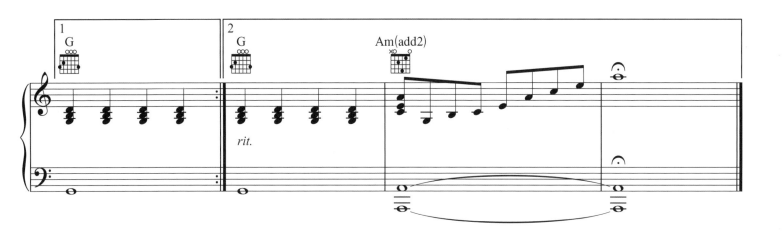

FOR BETTER OR WORSE

By PAUL CARDALL

Slowly, freely

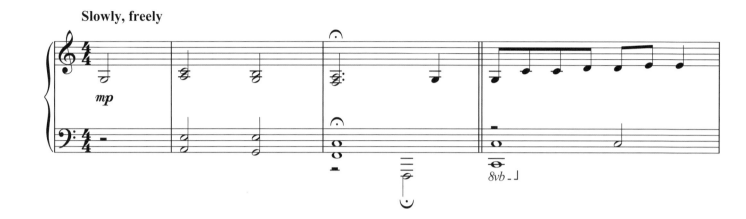

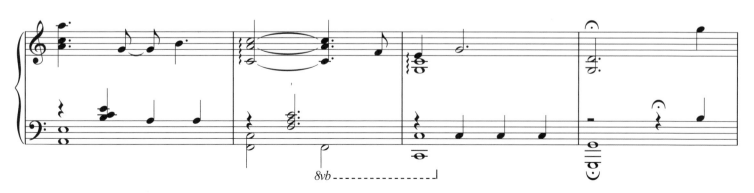

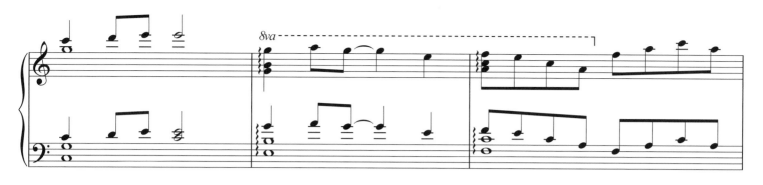

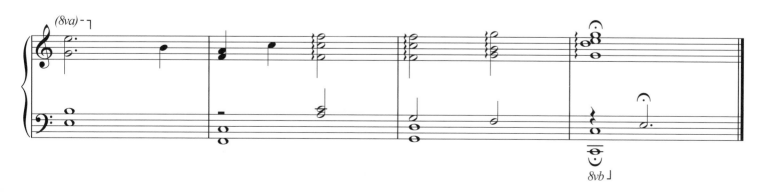

CHANGE

Words and Music by PAUL CARDALL
and TREVOR PRICE

So why are you try - ing to get me to change _____

when all of these feel - ings re - main __ the same? __

MY HEART BEATS FOR YOU

Words and Music by PAUL CARDALL,
JASON LANE and CRAIG WILSON

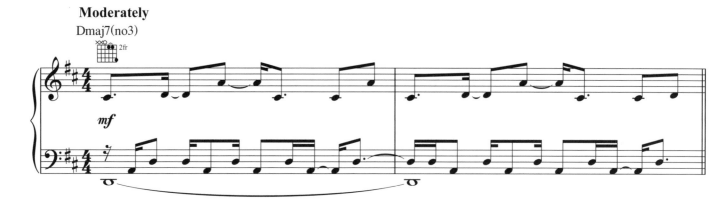

I will not — for-get — the day — I met — you.

Bro-ken down — in-side, — you walked — my way. — Like an

G A Bm

live for you ___ un - til ___ my life is through. ___ My

G A D

heart, it beats ___ for you. ___ My heart, ___ it beats ___ for you. ___ My heart, ___

Bm

To Coda ⊕

___ it beats ___ for you, ___ oh. ___ My heart, ___ it beats ___ for you. My heart, ___

D

___ it beats ___ for you, ___ oh. ___ The way you've learned ___ to love ___ me can't be eas -

I had all but thought my life was o - ver, look-ing at the years and what they gave. _ I was

stuck in a place, no way to es-cape, trapped by _ my shame. _

Oh. _ 'Cause I'm not the man _ that you once met. _

_ The day _ you stole _ my heart, _

SOME KIND OF WONDERFUL

Words and Music by PAUL CARDALL,
TY HERNDON and JOEL LINDSEY

TINA'S THEME

By PAUL CARDALL

FINDING MY WAY

By PAUL CARDALL

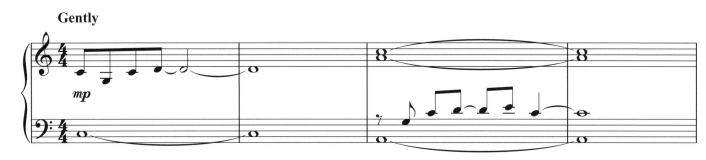

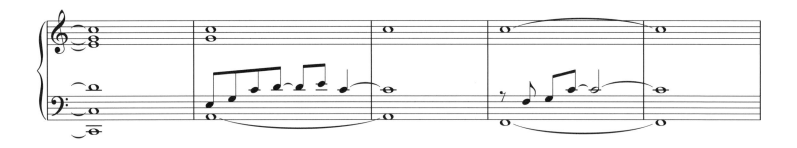

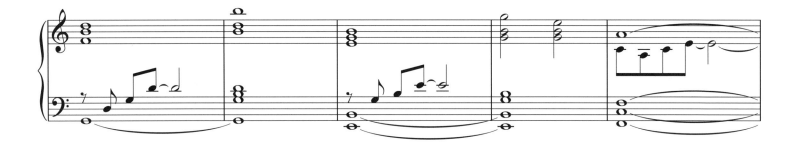

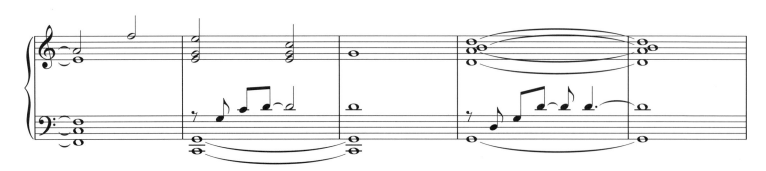

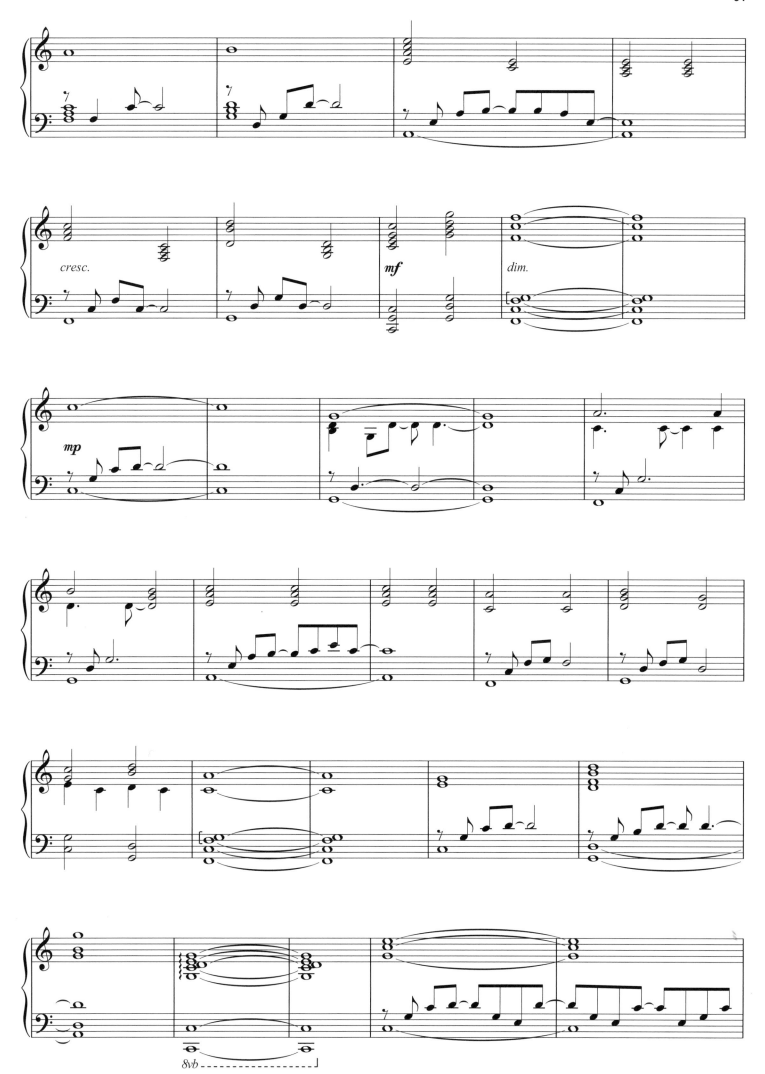

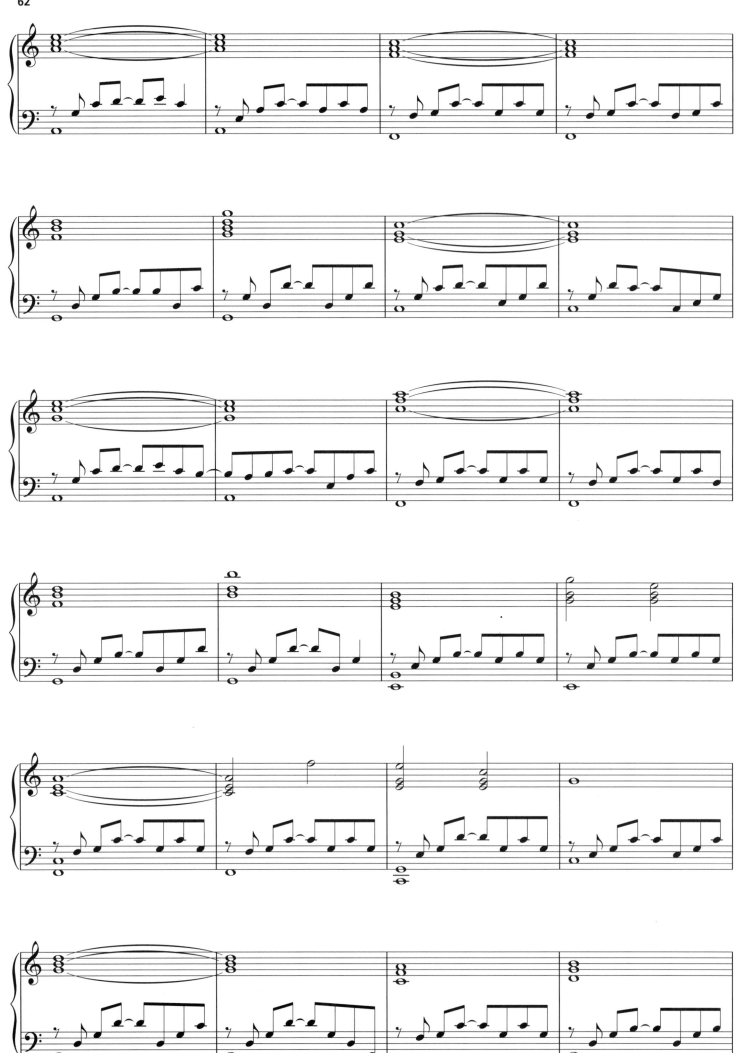

BROKEN MACHINE

Words and Music by PAUL CARDALL,
RACHAEL YAMAGATA and TREVOR PRICE

*Recorded a half step lower.

THE BROKEN MIRACLE

Words and Music by PAUL CARDALL,
MATT HAMMITT and CARTER FRODGE

WE COULD BE KIND

Words and Music by JOHN DAVID BRATTON
and ETHAN ROBERTS

Recorded a half step higher.

EPILOGUE

By PAUL CARDALL